HOUGHTON MIFFLIN

Reading

A Legacy of Literacy

Smart Solutions

HOUGHTON MIFFLIN

BOSTON • MORRIS PLAINS, NJ

California • Colorado • Georgia • Illinois • New Jersey • Texas

Design, Art Management and Page Production: Kirchoff/Wohlberg, Inc.

ILLUSTRATION CREDITS
4-21 Diane Hearn. **22-39** Bethann Thornburgh. **40-57** Michael Chesworth.

Printed in U.S.A.

ISBN: 0-618-04395-0

15 16 17 - VH - 06 05 04

Smart Solutions

Contents

Tall Tony

by Lucy Floyd

illustrated by
Diane Hearn

Strategy Focus

Tony is the tallest boy in his class, and
sometimes that's a bother. As you read,
evaluate how well the words and pictures
work together to tell Tony's story.

Tony was very tall. In fact, he was the tallest person in his class. He was even taller than the teacher, Ms. Bell.

Tony didn't mind being tall. He liked being able to reach things nobody else could reach.

Tony was always reaching up high for something.

"Tony, I need that book on the top shelf. Will you please get it for me?" Alex asked.

Tony got the book.

"Tony, it's hot in here. Will you please open that window?" May asked.

Tony opened the window.

"Tony, I want this elephant picture at the top of the board. Will you please tack it up for me?" Ms. Bell asked.

Tony tacked up the picture.

"Tony, I forgot to write *Canada* at the top of this map," Anna said. "Will you please write it for me?"

Tony wrote *Canada*.

Day after day, Tony had to do things because he was the tallest person in his class.

Who had to draw stars at the top of the mural?

Tony did.

Who had to measure the clock AND the door for math lesson?

Tony did.

One day, Tony got tired of doing all the reaching. "I'm going to shrink myself," he thought. "Being tall is driving me CRAZY. I've got to say something about it."

14

So Tony raised his hand.

"Yes, Tony?" said Ms. Bell.

"I want to say something to the class," Tony said.

"Later," said Ms. Bell. "Right now it's time to go to the gym for basketball."

In the gym, everyone gathered around Mr. Sams, the basketball coach.

"A basketball team needs a captain," he said. "Now, who do you think it should be?"

"The player who knows all about basketball!" said Alex.

"The player who is super fast!" said May.

"The player who is a good leader!" said Jim.

"The player who shoots lots of baskets!" said Anna.

"Who is that player?" asked Mr. Sams.

"Me!" said Tony, standing very straight to look as tall as he could. "How about me?"

"YES!" everybody yelled. "CAPTAIN TONY!"

"Now we can start practice," said Mr. Sams.

"But first, there's one thing I need you to do, Tony."

"Name it, Coach," said Tony happily.

"The basketball is on top of the shelf," said Mr. Sams. "Will you please reach up and get it for me?"

Responding

Think About the Selection

1. Who is taller than his teacher?

2. What problem does Alex have? How does he solve it?

Tony Finds Solutions

Copy the web on a piece of paper. Write Tony's problem in the circle. Write solutions to Tony's problem that you read about in the story.

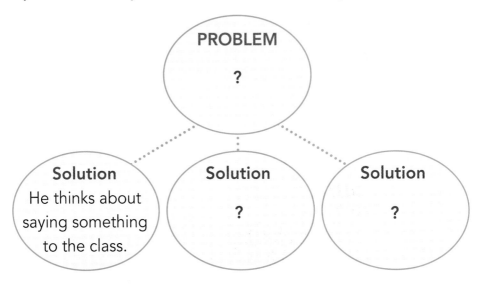

PROBLEM

?

Solution
He thinks about saying something to the class.

Solution

?

Solution

?

A Little Bit "Hotter" Can't Hurt

By Joanna Korba
Illustrated by Bethann Thornburgh

Strategy Focus

When Lindy visits Texas, Aunt Birdie makes chili. As you read, **predict** how *warm* a welcome the chili will be.

". . . in Texas!" Lindy Parker finished.

"Aunt Birdie and Uncle Buster are so glad we're coming," said her mother. "Birdie made some chili just for you."

"Is it hot like your chili?" Lindy asked.
"I *love* your chili!"

"The Grigsbees like their chili mild," her
mother said. "But be nice, honey. Pretend
you like it."

"We're so tickled to see y'all!" cried
Uncle Buster.

"I made some chili just for you, Lindy.
I know you love chili," said Aunt Birdie.
"Now give me some sugar!"

Lindy laughed and planted a kiss on her
aunt's cheek.

Lindy's mother whispered to her sister, "Lindy likes hot chili, Birdie. Can you make yours a bit hotter?"

"Well, sure," said Aunt Birdie. "A little bit hotter can't hurt."

It was a lazy afternoon in the Texas sun.
Everyone sat out front to talk. Aunt Birdie
went inside to get some iced tea.

The chili was cooking. Aunt Birdie walked
over and lifted the cover. Then she reached
for the chili powder.

"I'll add a little for Lindy," she said to
herself. "A little bit hotter can't hurt."

Aunt Birdie came back out. Buster was telling Lindy about the flowers on the lawn.

"Your Aunt Birdie won't let those flowers be cut down," he said. "So I just mow around them!"

After a while, Lindy's mother went to get a sweet potato pie from the oven. She saw the chili — and the chili powder.

"I'll make it a little bit hotter for Lindy," she thought. "Birdie said she didn't mind."

Later, Lindy played with the hens. Aunt Birdie and Uncle Buster kept them as pets.

"We will be eating dinner soon, Lindy," her mother said. "Give your hands a good washing."

Lindy washed her hands. Then she saw the chili and the chili powder.

"I'll make the chili just a little bit hotter," she thought. "I don't want to upset Aunt Birdie. But a little bit hotter can't hurt."

Everyone helped set the table. Then Aunt Birdie brought out the giant bowl of chili.

Lindy was worried. She had only added a *little* bit of chili powder. Would anyone notice?

Everyone took a bite of chili. Everyone's eyes got larger. You see, the chili wasn't a *little* bit hotter. . . .

It . . . was . . . a . . . LOT . . . hotter!

"But I only put in a little more chili powder!"
Aunt Birdie cried.

"Oh, dear," said Lindy's mother. "So did I!"

"Oh, no! Me too!" cried Lindy.

"Well! It's a good thing *I* didn't add some chili powder," said Uncle Buster. "Our smoke alarms would go off!"

"You know what?" said Aunt Birdie. "I like it this way!"

And from that day on, everyone in Lindy's family liked chili that was a little bit hotter.

Now that can't hurt, can it?

Think About the Selection

1 What food does Aunt Birdie say she made just for Lindy?

2 What three clues let you know that there is a lot of chili powder in the chili?

Use Clues to Draw a Conclusion

Copy the chart on a piece of paper. Then complete the chart by writing two more clues about the weather that day.

Clues

?

Everyone sits out front to talk.

?

Conclusion

The story takes place on a hot day.

The Dive

by Susan Delaney
illustrated by Michael Chesworth

Strategy Focus

Christy won't admit it, but she is scared to learn to dive. As you read, stop now and then to **summarize** what you've read so far.

Christy had waited all week for Megan's party at the public pool. And it was turning out to be lots of fun.

Christy showed everyone how to do a split jump.

She was just about to do a twist in the air. Then Sara arrived.

Sara could dive. And everyone wanted to learn.

For the rest of the day, the pool was filled with the sound of the girls hitting the water on their bellies like little whales. By the end of the day, everyone had tried to dive. Everyone but Christy.

When she got home, Christy lay on her bed,
thinking about the party. Diving is silly anyway,
she thought. Who wants to plop into the water
headfirst, like a frog?

But she started doing pretend dives anyway. She puffed out her cheeks and swung her arms back. Just then, her brother walked in.

When he saw Christy, he began to laugh. "What are you, some kind of blowfish?" he asked.

Christy gave him a look that said, "Very funny."
Then she asked, "Hey, Nathan, do you know how
to dive?"

"Sure. Diving is easy," Nathan replied. He put his
hands together and jumped onto Christy's bed.
Then Nathan saw the hurt look on her face.

"I can help you," he said. Nathan showed her how
to hold her arms and bend her legs.

Before dinner, Christy told her mom about the party. "Sara ruined it," she said. "She thinks she's so great because she knows how to dive."

Her mom gave her a funny look. "I thought you liked Sara," she said.

"I guess she's okay," Christy admitted. "But I don't like diving."

"Did you even try?" asked her mom.

"I can't!" Christy whined. "I hold my nose when I jump. You can't hold your nose and dive."

"You have to blow air out your nose," her mother said. She showed Christy what to do.

Christy thought her mom looked like a snorting dragon when she blew air out her nose. Christy decided to practice in front of a mirror before she tried it in public.

The next day, Christy, her mom, and Nathan
headed for the town pool. When they got there,
Sara was waiting for them.

"Hi Christy," Sara said. "Want to practice diving together? Then maybe you can show me your split jump."

"Umm, okay," Christy said. She was still afraid.

"The first time I tried diving, I was really scared," said Sara, as if she could read Christy's mind. "But finally I closed my eyes and just dived right in. It was easy after that."

Then Christy's mom, and Nathan, and Sara all stood beside her at the edge of the pool. Suddenly, Christy didn't feel afraid!

Nathan raised his hands, and Christy raised her
hands. Christy's mother blew air out her nose, and
Christy blew air out her nose. Sara smiled. She
dived in. And Christy dived in right after her.

Responding

Think About the Selection

1 Who could do a real dive?

2 The story says that Christy waited all week for Megan's party. Tell what you think *all week* means.

What Does It Mean?

Copy the chart on a piece of paper. Write what each generalization from the story really means.

Generalization	What It Means
Christy showed *everyone* how to do a split jump.	Christy showed everyone at Megan's party how to do a split jump.
Diving is silly anyway, she thought.	?
"Diving is easy," Nathan replied.	?

57